Tricia Harris
CA8 9JY
UK

ISBN: 978-1-008-99917-6
Imprint: Lulu.com

A DIPPER FLEW PAST, CALLING

A YEAR AT WOODY GLEN
BOOK ONE
2017-18

TRICIA HARRIS

PICTURES BY RICHARD HARRIS

INTRODUCTION

NOT A DAY goes by when I don't realise how lucky I am to live where I do – in a beautiful house in a lovely village and, most of all, with a garden which has become our own private Cumbrian nature reserve.

The part of our garden that is cultivated is more than most people can dream of, with all kinds of birds – everything from goldfinches and siskin to woodpeckers and long-tailed tits – coming to the feeders that hang outside our kitchen and bedroom windows.

But beyond that garden we have nearly three acres of woodland – oaks, sycamores, birch, beech and rowan, and a very unusual understory of holly – with a stream known as Hawkey Beck tumbling gently though it.

Here we find even more varieties of birds – buzzards in the trees and dippers along the beck – as well as roe deer, badgers and all kinds of rodents.

In the 30 years we have lived here at Woody Glen I have seen 84 species of birds – either in or flying above our land.

I had kept informal records but had never bothered to do any more . . . until, at the April meeting of my Book Club, the conversation turned to the fact that although I kept talking about writing a book about Woody Glen's wildlife I never actually did anything about it. My friend Linda, who we bought the house from more than 30 years ago and is now a keen member of the Book Club, was –

not surprisingly – beginning to lose patience.

'Just get on with it!' she said.

So this time I came home on a mission: To record more formally the huge variety of wildlife I am privileged to watch and listen to in my garden. This is the result . . .

BLUE TIT

April 12: I came home from my book club determined to start the book I had been talking about for so long – which is why it starts not on New Year's Day, or on the first day of spring, but today, in the middle of April.

When I got home I was delighted to hear a tawny owl up by the barn owl box. I gave a quick flash of the torch. I think at least one was inside.

Earlier in the day, on the cabin veranda in an hour from 3pm, I saw at least 20 species – the usual ones, plus a blackcap and a sparrowhawk. All went very quiet when he/she passed!

The primroses are out and I watched a bumblebee feeding in a fritillary near the garden pond.

There is a jackdaw possibly investigating a hole in the oak behind the silver birch, whose leaves are just at that magical dusting of pale spring green.

April 13: I shooed a jackdaw from the barn owl box. The woodpecker is drumming on the hill, a slightly metallic sound but I have not yet found out yet what he is using to make it. There are at least three in the wood. The males are busy courting a female, drumming and calling busily down by Hawkey Beck. The dipper is back again this spring, flying noisily up and downstream and often pausing to bob on the stone bridge before flying into the tunnel where the beck flows under the railway. They can use the same site for many years so they could well have nested in the tunnel since the Victorians built it.

We saw swallows arriving and geese leaving at the Steamboat Inn on the north Solway coast.

The rooks seem to have survived last night's storm of wind and rain and have been busy adding bits to their nests. I keep meaning to count and see how big the rookery is this year. There are a few new ones.

April 14: A damp and drizzly start to the day. Very few birds were around till it brightened up. I think there could be at least four blackcaps singing, but I have not heard a willow warbler yet. The first martin flew over the house, but I don't think he lingered. The chiffchaff has been going strong since March 14 and has now been joined by at least two more males.

The primroses are stunning this year – all from three small plants given to me by my mother-in-law about 25 years ago.

The roe deer is being picked up on the wildlife camera down below the badger sett. Her twins from last year seem to have moved on now.

I was about to go out of the front door when a chiffchaff came around the corner and busied itself hunting the pots for food. A glorious little bird. I've never seen one so close. I can understand why ornithologists didn't realise the willow warbler was a distinct species until it was identified by the different song!

It's drizzling again, and quite chilly.

April 15: The bird cherry is in full flower, bobbing happily in a chilly breeze but catching the sunshine beautifully. The rowan leaves are about to burst out, another stunning shade to add to the spectacle.

Wood sorrel is beginning to flower and the marsh marigolds, or kingcups if you prefer, are popping up in various new spots by the beck, including on a tiny island in a pool below the Valentine bridge.

The bridge has been moved and modified, but got the name as the original version was completed one Valentine's day.

The stone bridge, our first crossing built nearly 30 years ago with slabs 'walked' from the garden and slid down the banks on ladders, is currently dammed with winter flood debris, so the diversion under the adjacent black plank bridge is flowing well.

There is evidence of digging out under the bark of the dead Scots pine over this bridge. I shall keep an eye on it in case it is the tree creeper's nest. I have only realised recently what a sweet little song this bird has. I need to learn to recognise it better.

The roe buck has posed well for the bottom camera. I must check more often now. It would be good to see if he has any competition down there. They start to establish territory in May . . .

April 16: It's a wet, miserable morning with sudden showers so I am being lazy and sitting by the conservatory window. It is handy for chasing the pair of jackdaws from the veranda of the barn owl box but I suspect I won't be much of a deterrent.

I was rewarded by the blue tit, who is starting to build in the box on the wall of the house, and amused by a female blackbird sending debris flying out of the gutter above my head, possibly while looking for damp leaves to mould into the lining for her nest. She seems to be building in the top of a (no longer) dwarf conifer on the bank.

There is a tree creeper scurrying up the bark of the old birch, our favourite tree in the wood. It is a positively majestic tree and we love watching it throughout the seasons.

April 18: A frost this morning. Water is frozen in various pots but the pond is all right, and the tadpoles seem to be fine. The rooks are very noisy today, and flying around a lot. I'm not sure what stage their eggs or young are at. The parents carry food in a pouch under the beak so it is not obvious when they are feeding their young.

Woodpeckers are drumming almost constantly in various parts of the wood. Probably it's just two males flying from place to place but it's still very dramatic. I've still not heard a willow warbler. There's still time, I suppose.

GREAT SPOTTED
WOODPECKER

April 19: The blue tit in the box on the wall has just struggled in with an enormous bundle of our hair trimmings. That should make it very cosy. The robin looks the worse for wear, with lots of feathers missing or broken on his breast, but it looks as if he has seen his rival off as he is singing happily from one of the conifers on the bank. A dunnock is singing near him. They are nesting in the low lonicera hedge by the path. It looks as if the blackbird has finished building, so watch this space.

April 21: At last, there has been one brief song from the willow warbler, down in the southwest corner of the wood. He'd probably just arrived and staked his claim, and was then having a feed and a rest. I also saw another house martin, flying in the space over the railway line. I hope he is a local resident and won't just head on north.

A pair of nuthatches have been very busy, bustling up and down the oak in front of the cabin. In the wood there were some noisy woodpeckers, and some jackdaws that I chased away from the tawny owl box.

A pair of blue sutits have been feeding each other on the feeder, and coal tits have been bravely coming on to the veranda handrail. There have been a pair of great tits too, and a lone long–tailed tit (hopefully its mate is sitting on eggs, possibly down in the holly near the badger sett).

April 22: There was a swallow singing on a building in Carlisle Cathedral Close today. It sounded like summer though there is still a chill in the air and frost in the mornings.

Back in the wood I have decided to give in to the jackdaws as I feel that if the owls were going to set up home there they would have done so by now.

There was drama down at the cabin this afternoon. First the crows were flying in an amazing joint attack to attempt to chase the resident buzzard away. Then in a silence that I should have noticed sooner the sparrowhawk flew up into the canopy of a nearby beech with a small bird in its talons. I'm not sure what it

CUCKOO FLOWER

was. Hopefully it wasn't the willow warbler. I will keep listening.

April 24: Yesterday we saw a great flying display by sand martins at the confluence of the North and South Tyne. It felt as if summer had come.

How wrong can we be? There's a freezing north wind today, with sunshine, but also some hail and a frost warning for tonight. We have been covering what we can, but the wind is not making it easy.

I planted out all our self set cowslip plugs. They look as if they have always been there, especially the ones among the cuckoo flowers in the 'meadow' on the lawn.

The blackbird is feeding young, but I didn't manage to see if this is the family in the conifer. It was helping in the garden down there so it may be down in the holly.

April 26: At least two willow warblers are singing in the wood. They obviously waited until the icy blast from the north had passed through.

A lot of frost damage has been done to tender flowers and shrub tips. I've never seen laurel so scorched. No wonder flowers, and probably some fruit blossom, are so ravaged. I'm glad I took some garden photos a few days ago.

Another blackbird has just started to sing by the house, competing well with the blackcap in the laurel, and the song thrush is in the apple tree.

At least four blackcaps are in the wood, and similarly the chiffchaff. I need to listen at dawn soon to count more accurately. Maybe when it has warmed up a bit.

A large chunk of the holly at the bottom of the garden has snapped off. It had been dead for a while, supported by ivy, but frost and north wind has been too much for it.

Even the pink geranium, a tough plant, looks as if a large animal has rolled on it where it has been caught by the freezing gale.

Hopefully the weather will warm up over the weekend and encourage the bluebells to come out fully. The primroses are past their best now, but at least the cowslips and cuckoo flower are still lovely.

MAY

May 2: We have been away further north and returned to see that the foliage on everything has come on tremendously despite the cold wind that appears to be still here. The jackdaws look rather settled in the barn owl box. Never mind. It was warm enough to eat supper in the garden on the new table that arrived while we were away. There was lots of 'chat' from the rookery, and darkness fell with the song thrush in full voice outside our window. Heavenly!

May 3: There are fledged rooks outside the nest, hanging on for dear life in the gale. But at least it is dry. I can see only one pair of baby rooks so far, so I can only hope the bad weather hasn't affected the rest too badly. The jackdaw is still building in the owl box. I wonder why they seem to nest much later than other members of the crow family.Talking of owl boxes, there is a starling family in the little owl box in the Scots pine by the house, and possibly tree sparrows in the box containing the camera on the neighbouring silver birch.

The cow parsley down the lane has gone from green buds to white flowers in a day. We have had lovely warm sun despite the still chilly wind.

May 4: There is still a cold east wind, but it's very dry for Cumbria in May. A song thrush is being followed around by at least one healthy youngster. I found a splendid rooks' nest that had blown down. What an amazing piece of bird architecture it is! There was no obvious sign of eggs or young, so I'm not sure it had even been used. There was an amusing moment viewed from the cabin when a young pigeon was joined on a small branch by a parent. The branch snapped with an audible crack. Fortunately the youngster could fly!

A young chaffinch was begging for food under the feeder, but the father just ignored it and it soon started to eat by itself.

I checked the wildcam at the bottom again. There were lots of new photos so I must catalogue the dates soon. The batteries have lasted for ages this time so I haven't brought the memory card up to transfer the photos. There are 850 at the moment!

May 5: Two young rooks have managed to fly from the Scots pine to a neighbouring silver birch, sitting very close together, and hanging on tight as it's still quite windy.

JACKDAW

Last night we had a roll cloud – a Volutus, a very rare phenomenon – right over the house. It looked like a giant bolster and was rather beautiful. It is a variation of the Helm cloud, caused by our local wind, the Helm Wind (the only British wind which has its own name.)

I was hopeful that a stock dove was nesting in one of the random boxes I made last year out of offcuts from the cabin, but I realised it was just a young wood pigeon sitting on the top looking for his parents to feed him.

The jays are nesting in some dense ivy in a tree below the bottom of the duck run.

The greatest excitement of the day was spotting the roe doe down near the stream, digging through the leaves with her feet, at around 10 in the morning. The wildcam had picked her and the buck up last night, and then I saw her myself on the opposite bank about an hour later. There was a dipper sitting in my way on the bridge as well. I never did finish my planned lap of the garden.

May 6: The goldcrest was attacking its reflection in the office window today. I'm fairly certain it is nesting in the Scots pine on the lawn as it frequently sings from there. The great tit is still sometimes attacking the bedroom window, but it must be busy with young now as it is not so noisy.

The dunnocks are busy in the shrubs on the bank. There is another nest there, I think. I'm still searching for the woodpecker hole in the wood. They are possibly not feeding yet. It will be easier to spot when they are.

There was a great cacophony at the top of the hill this evening. Lots of rook and crow families have fledged today, and they have been vying for air and perching space. The nesting jackdaws have joined in as well.

May 7: The deer has been very busy stirring up the leaves. They both give birth and rut in May so I'm not sure what part of their lives the leaf clearing is part of. I will try to find out. The tree creeper is very busy gathering food near the beck. I am fairly certain there is a nest in the old pine over the stone bridge.

Great excitement! There was a heron footprint in the mud down by the beck. I have seen one patrolling the water from time to time but not for a while.

The bluebells are particularly good this year. We felled a couple of tall thin sycamores for firewood last year and all the wildflowers are enjoying the extra light.

The wood sorrel has had a good year too. We are hoping the log stacks have provided some nest sites. I will sit downthere in a day or two to see if there is any evidence.

I have put a dustbin lid of mud at the front of the house, hoping the few house martins we have will spot it and use the mud to personalise the artificial nests on the front of the house. It's worth a try.

The tree sparrows are feeding young in one end of the sparrow terrace nest box on the front of the house, and there's a family in the hanging nest box opposite it.

The jackdaws in the tawny owl box in the wood are feeding young and getting rather noisy! I've no idea where the nuthatch is nesting, though I see one of them most days on the fat feeder near the cabin.

May 8: It's still chilly in the mornings, but it's dry – probably too dry for the time of the year.

It's so dry it's hard for the birds to find food for their young.

Richard has managed to get the camera in the bird box working after a break of three years or more. The camera inside the box has moved so there is no picture. But there is lots of noise made by the tree sparrows, which is rather exciting.

There were none here when we came 27 years ago but we have quite a colony now. The nuthatch wasn't here then either but they arrived about 15 years ago, and we now have at least two pairs nesting.

The swifts have arrived in the next village, but I have not seen them here yet.

The sparrowhawk was soaring over the garden earlier, but it can't have been seen, or perceived as a threat, as the blackbird just kept on singing!

May 9: The cold wind has at last died down to a breeze, but it is still very chilly. The tree sparrows in the box keep knocking the camera so we are hoping they will move it enough for us to get a picture as the babies grow a bit more. It sounds as if there are at least three in there.

The young jackdaws sound as if they are doing well, but I don't think the ones in the owl box near the house have hatched yet. The starlings in the remaining owl box on the lawn are thriving. They are getting very noisy so I think we are likely to see them soon.

May 10: We were away from home today, with the kayaks on Ullswater. It was a glorious day, with very little wind so we had a good paddle across the lake from Glencoyne. There were sandpipers on the island, and Canada geese probably nesting, so we didn't land because we did not want to disturb them. Other people were not so considerate! We went to the south of the lake, pausing to listen, mainly for the cuckoo, which is increasingly rare up here.

We were amazed to see that the river that comes through Glenridding was not visible above the bed as it enters the lake, so it's hard to believe it is the same one that did so much terrible damage in the floods in 2015. A long pause in a calm stretch by Seldom Seen finally gave us a couple of cuckoo calls, and as we reloaded the car the hills at last echoed with calls.

May 11: There's a real summer feel to the day today. There is very little wind, and what there is is from the southwest at last, which is much better. The tree creeper was scuttling up the oak opposite the cabin with a beak full of food, but I didn't see which way he went with it. The woodpecker seems more active again, so tomorrow I will try to find where he is nesting as it looks like he has mouths to feed.

There have been a few queen wasps around recently. One keeps trying to get into the house and a second has been investigating under the cabin roof. I will discourage both options. I do let them survive if possible though as they are great pest destroyers and only become pesky themselves when they get dozy at the end of the season.

The great excitement is that one of the long-tailed tit families have fledged. They were in the apple tree, flitting about, so it was hard to count them. But there were probably at least five young.

May 12: They may be the same family as I saw yesterday, but hopefully the long-tailed tits from down by the cabin have also fledged. They were too high in the canopy to count!

The roe buck has made another appearance on the wildcam, and looks as if he has either been chewing, or cleaning his antlers on the snakebark maple that Richard gave me years ago. It gets eaten, and crushed by falling branches, yet still manages to survive!

Two squirrels dashed through the trees as I was going down the back of the hill. With the sun on them they briefly looked like reds, but I think that was very unlikely. I didn't see them again, sadly, but will keep looking out.

The bluebells are still stunning, and smell gorgeous in the morning sunshine.

The first swift has come at last, cruising the sky over the house, along with a house martin. Let's hope the latter spots the mud in the dustbin lid and puts it to good use.

There is potential success in a couple of the bird boxes. I have been worrying that the cold weather has caused a shortage of caterpillars, so I was delighted this afternoon to see a blue tit taking food into our oldest box – the one that we moved from the magnificent birch by the house, down to an oak at the bottom corner of the duck run.

Also the broken swift box that Richard converted has a great tit family in it. It is situated on another oak near the steps down to the lower level of the wood.

I have seen a spotted flycatcher at last, flying out from a dead branch over the bank below theduck run. We have put a new box up for it this year as the old one fell apart. I usually see the first one by the house.

May 13: We woke up to the first rain for weeks, which will be very welcome for ground feeding birds. I suspect the worms have been a long way down. The song thrush certainly sounds appreciative; he was singing a lot this morning in the south west corner of the wood.

There is a magpie down by the beck, being mobbed by a blackbird. We don't see them very often – we're more likely to see crows and jays. Also there has been a lone long-tailed tit collecting food, so maybe the brood in the bottom of the wood haven't fledged yet.

It is much easier to walk quietly now the rain has dampened down the dry leaves. Any bare patch of ground that gets daylight is covered with a dusting of tiny seedlings, mainly foxgloves, encouraged by the rain.

There are also dozens of two-inch high trees, mostly sycamore, but with some ash, rowan, birdcherry, beech and oak.

Back up near the house the bluetits in the wall box are busy feeding young. The goldcrest is still bouncing at the office window and the tree sparrows are still making a lot of noise in the camera box.

May 14: I woke at 4.30 and realised the dawn chorus was really getting going. My first instinct was to get up and go down to the cabin, but I didn't – partly because I realised that would disturb a lot of wildlife and partly because I was so nice and cosy. So my brilliant compromise was to open the curtains, and the outside door in our bedroom and listen from there.

It was early enough for the tawny owl to be still calling, which, heard against the fantastic

NUTHATCH

bird song from all around, was lovely. In fact it was so loud it was almost impossible to identify the various species. Incredibly special!

In the afternoon while walking at Gilsland on the Northumberland border Val and I saw a roe buck very close. He paused in his grazing on the banks of the River Irthing to watch us, but he must have been very aware of where the path went as the only movements he made was a bit of ear twitching and turning his head to look down to the river where there were some noisy children playing happily in the water. A magical moment which proves they are quite happy to be out in full daylight if they are not disturbed.

May 15: I went for a short walk to listen to the dawn chorus, even though it is very hard to identify the different birds. Certainly there are a lot of blackbirds this year, which is good as they had a poor year last year.

The robin is the loudest by the window but with such a variety of species, and many of the same species, it is hard to define any pattern or order to it. Interestingly I couldn't hear the blackcaps. Maybe they prefer to sing in the daytime.

The promised rain arrived at eight o'clock.

It remained a gloomy day with some showers but, with more food being around to feed the young, the dampness encouraged a lot of bird activity. A baby long-tailed tit was hanging precariously on a clematis stem, reluctant to follow the foraging family. The blue tits on the wall are feeding frantically, as are the ones on the Scots pine at the front of the house.

May 16: The dawn chorus sounded louder than ever, maybe because they had eaten well the day before. It's generally warmer today, but quite windy again, though it's quitepleasant as the wind is from the southwest rather than the east. The beck is back to normal level for the time of year, and there was no need for me to top up the frog pond this morning. There are a few tadpoles in there but it is really too full of flag irises now to make a good frog habitat. I will try to clear some out at the end of the summer.

There are blue tits in the box near the hens that is hanging rather precariously by the bottom screw. I hope it lasts, though I'm glad we didn't disturb them by trying to mend it.
.I saw a few white butterflies and plenty of midges in the evening but hope we get some others soon. There are not many bees yet either, mainly lone bumbles.

One of the nuthatches is taking food to the southwest corner of the wood. I think he crosses the beck but he flies so fast and varies his route so it is hard to work out exactly where he is nesting.

I saw the grey squirrel again today, just cheekily taking food to the top of one of my homemade empty bird boxes and sitting there to eat it. We do miss our reds who were a total delight and very tame.

May 17: Another dry bright day. I went to Dalemain (a beautiful country house near Ullswater) with Judy and we both agreed the shortage of bees in the garden, and generally, was a grave concern. There were a few bumbles on the comfrey in particular, and one or two smaller bees, but we didn't see a single honey bee.

We found great delight watching the house martins collecting mud in the stable yard, though. They were just beginning their nests in the top of the windows. What amazing architecture, and alldone with just a beak! Apparently they don't carry the mud in the beak, they balance it on top.

Back home the activity in all the nest boxes is getting frenetic. I think most will be empty in the next day or two. A neighbour chased a woodpecker off one of them. It's lucky I have metal guards round some of the entrance holes.

May 18: The first tortoiseshell butterfly of the year – and a few honey bees on the cotoneaster. It is a bit warmer today so hopefully things will improve from now on.

May 19: There's some very loud cheeping from the webcam box – it sounds as if only one baby tree sparrow is in there now, so maybe the others have flown. A parent comes back occasionally but doesn't seem to be feeding it, and there is a lot of practice fluttering going on, so leaving seems imminent. It will probably happen when I look away!

Val and I sat in the wood hoping to see the long-tailed tit family but the only sighting was high in the canopy. There was plenty to watch and listen to though, and the female roe deer had posed for the wildcam.

The tree sparrows are still in their box! As are the blue tits and great tits in theirs. They must all be going very soon though.

May 20: Typically, the long-tailed tit family were outside the bedroom window this morning, but I had no chance to count them because they were just moving on as I drew the curtains. There was a lot of calling so it sounded a good number.

The tree sparrows were still in their box, but by ten o'clock I thought they had flown. But no! They must have been asleep. They are still in there and cheeping louder than ever this evening. None of the blue or great tits have gone either. They will probably go tomorrow when I'm not around to see it.

ORANGE TIP BUTTERFLY

I think the grey squirrel is demolishing my coconut feeders in the wood. I have tried to make the feeders more secure, and have set the old webcam to see if I can catch the squirrels in the act. Unfortunately I can't alter the settings on it now so I can't have it on all day. We shall see.

May 21: The tree sparrows have moved the nest around so the camera is now pointing in the right direction and we can see them! There are at least four babies.

I went with the Geltsdale fellwalkers for a walk up the higher reaches of the South Tyne valley today. It's still cool for the time of year but mainly dry. The song and mistle thrushes were all singing well, and we surprised a roe buck in a new mixed wood. There has been lots of tree planting up there, which is excellent.

I heard very few curlew, peewit or oystercatchers, and only possibly one faint cuckoo. The wildflowers were excellent though and we passed through many old hay meadows. I saw my first mallard ducklings of the year – five about a month old, then seven, probably only a couple of days old.

I came home to find the sparrows in the box were now easily seen – four young, one of them much smaller than the others but still very lively.

May 22: All but one of the tree sparrows flew by nine o'clock this morning. The parents keep coming back to it to try to get the one to join the others that had flown but they had had no luck by lunchtime. They have continued to feed it, and chivvy it to the exit but it won't take the final leap. One parent often just sits with it while the other calls from outside, it is an amazing bond considering they have three other mouths to feed.

The south west corner of the wood is very busy today, with lots of young blackbirds begging for food, a willow warbler, blackcap and chiffchaff all singing well and a wren trying to drown them out. Gorgeous. Then the buzzard started calling above them. I'm fairly sure its nest is down there this year.

The nettles are growing fast, and already have signs of insects making their homes on them. I've seen a lot of red soldier beetles today on and near the stumpery, some of them drying their wings so they look newly hatched.

The baby tree sparrow was still in the box in the evening, but one parent came in to brood it overnight so it still has a chance.

May 23: The box is empty! So the parent knew that even though this chick was by far the smallest it had a good chance of fledging successfully. Nature at its best.

A lovely willow warbler is singing in the garden today. Maybe the cold winds seriously delayed their migration this year, as we now have three or four singing. It's a glorious morning, with warm sun, a gentle breeze, and a very blue sky. Perfect.

May 24: It's a very still morning and pleasantly warm and wonderfully quiet, with no human noise at all. The birds are not making much sound either but two blackbirds are singing sporadically. One is very much a novice, though he has raised a family. His song is very limited, with only a couple of short phrases. The chaffinch is singing his heart out in the apple tree. One thing I find fascinating about them is their song has a local accent. Experts would no doubt recognise him as an Eden Valley resident.

I have a new seat by the log store and many birds rarely notice me here. A dunnock has just been bustling around looking for food right in front of me.

It was so quiet today that I thought I heard a cuckoo in the distance, but since we haven't heard one here for many years I think it was unlikely. Our local tawny owl was calling during the day again, but we are so used to that I don't think I was confused by it.

We have a very tame male blackbird that helps with the gardening. He is feeding young. It is amazing how much he can fit in his beak, and even sing a short song with his mouth full, before taking it to the nestlings.

May 25: I was in the garden early. It was very damp and misty but with a promise of a lovely day. The scent is very powerful on days like these, and the semi wild azaleas and the violas are particularly wonderful.

We visited what will be our final resting place – a nearby woodland and meadow burial ground. It was a perfect day for it as the sun came out and there was just a faint breeze. Lots of willow warblers were singing, which was a great delight, and many other resident and migrant birds were around. There was a huge variety of grasses, interspersed with buttercup, vetch and plantain (a really beautiful underrated flower) which filled the meadow with other

SPOTTED FLYCATCHER

delights not far from flowering, and the may blossom on the perimeter hedge was stunning.

Back home in our wood it sounded as if the great tits in the converted swift box were about to fledge as there was a lot of noise there. Then I realised they'd spotted a neighbour's cat shinning up the trunk of the oak tree. A well aimed empty half coconut shell soon discouraged him.

There was then more drama as a crow chased something large through the lower canopy – either a rival crow or a buzzard, but it happened so fast it was difficult to say. I also saw the squirrel again. With the sun on it it looked reddish so it raised our hopes, but it was almost certainly the grey.

The jackdaws are still in the tawny owl box. I have no idea how many there are but they are very noisy. They are not being fed so frequently so I presume they are getting larger portions. The pair in the barn owl box started breeding a bit later so they are still being fed often, but they are getting noisier by the day so it probably won't be long till both sets fly.

I've just spotted another blue tit nest, in the fork of an oak. They nested there last year so I

have kept an eye on it, but they have built, and obviously part raised their young without my noticing them. That takes this year's tally up to at least six. I'll check other sites that I thought hadn't been used.

It was such a lovely warm evening that we sat looking out over the wood until nearly nine o'clock hoping to spot the deer. Then, sitting up by the house, I enjoyed a spectacular air show from our bats. They breed in the roof. I think they are all pipistrelles of some sort, but one day I will get my promised bat detector and find out for sure.

May 26: Another very warm day. I rescued lots of honey bees from the conservatory, as well as the first red admiral butterfly of the year. I also had to rescue a great tit from our shower room. No doubt he had come in the window to catch spiders.

SPOTTED FLYCATCHER

May 27: The various birds seem to still be in their boxes Maybe they are waiting until after the rain which is forecast today. There have been more honey bees – joined by at least two species of small bumble bee and the large one – enjoying the geranium phaem which has seeded itself everywhere.

The storm broke while I was down in the Lake District. It was scary to watch how quickly the rivers rose. Places flooded in 2015 be holding their breath. It was all very local though. Lots of water was running down from the Kirkstone area where the storm was at its height, but further down Ullswater the streams were still fairly quiet.

May 28: We left Cumbria to travel south to Gloucester. The rain had freshened up the countryside and the further we drove the greener it became – more the solid green of summer than the huge varieties of the green of late spring.

May 29: Gloucestershire was glorious and very English, including the steady rain that fell all day. As we drove back north the skies lightened and the roads dried up. It was good to be home.

May 30: It feels as if we have been away for a while. The rain has brought full summer here too. I wondered if the bird boxes would be empty as we had heard flocks of feeding families of tits further south, but some of ours still have occupants. The jackdaws haven't fledged yet, and nor have all the blue tits. I think the great tits in the swift box have gone though, as have their near neighbours, the blue tits, in the old box at the corner of the duck run.

May 31: There were baby blue tits peeping out of the box on the Scots pine, and a lot of activity in the one on the house wall. Two hours later the Scots pine family had gone, and I think the others were gone too by the time we came home in the afternoon.

Today we took the kayaks to Derwentwater and paddled up the Derwent to Grange. We heard a cuckoo over Lodore, and passed sand martin nests in the bank. There were lots of tiny goslings, barnacle and Canada, but none of the young mergansers I was expecting.

A lot of herons were around as well, so I must check to see if there is a heronry round there. Some very noisy sandpipers and oystercatchers were on the low islands at the mouth of the river, which was teeming with tiny fish.

I looked at the webcam box. The nest seems to have been rebuilt so we can't see inside again, but it will be lovely to have another brood.

The blue tit was still in the fork of the oak this morning, and the jackdaws still in the tawny owl box. We will see what tomorrow brings.

JUNE

June 1: The box on the house wall still had the family in it. They started to leave at lunchtime; two or three flew while we were eating but one changed his mind at the last minute and we wondered if he would be deserted. But an hour later the parents started to feed him again. There may be two in there as an adult flew out with sacs of poo in quick succession. The jackdaws were very noisy today, but I have not seen any faces yet so fledging is not imminent.

Lots more small bumblebees are enjoying the garden, and a red admiral has been sunning itself on the garden bench. Also there are plenty of aphids crawling around so there will be an abundance of food for all.

June 2: There are still at least two young in the box on the wall. One nearly left at lunchtime but decided getting his second shoulder through was rather scary, so the parents had to continue to feed them.

I've planted lots of the small white comfrey near the geranium phaem at the woodland edge. It should be appreciated by the bees next year. They have been enjoying a cardoon I planted last year in the garden. I'm delighted that we seem to have a lot of bumbles and honeybees now.

Down in the wood in the late afternoon the song thrush was singing beautifully. One evening last year he sang right into the night. The blue tits are still in residence in the oak tree, as are the jackdaws above them.

A large branch of beech has finally come down. It had been balanced by a thread since earlier in the year and the leaves even came out!

I was about to go into the house when I spotted a squirrel going up the oak where the jackdaws are. It went straight past the box but when it was about ten feet above it the parent bird went for it. The squirrel retaliated and there was a bit of a tussle, then it climbed higher. When it came back down the same happened, and then the jackdaw followed it as it crossed into a beech. It returned the same way, but passed the box without hesitating and came down to the ground. The other parent jackdaw immediately fed the young. It had obviously been waiting until the danger had passed.

June 3: On a lovely drive to Edinburgh the trees further north were mainly still in their more colourful spring greens.

June 4: The garden looks as if we have been away for a week, not just one night. Everything seems to have grown massively, and there are new things in flower, including a splendid orchid in the 'hay meadow'. I bought it from a wildflower stall at Haltwhistle last year and am delighted it has flourished. The wild parsnip is looking well too.

June 5: It's very quiet now that the blue tits have fledged, but the jackdaws are still in their boxes. Showers have brought out the midges so there is not too much sitting and watching the wildlife today. I heard a curlew calling over the fields, a joy to hear as they are getting rather scarce round here now. The song thrush has sung nearly all day, and the blackbirds have been helping in the garden – another family to feed I think.

June 6: Very heavy rain and strong winds all day. I'm hoping it hasn't affected the wildlife too badly.

June 7: It's very wet underfoot and a lot of the vegetation is dashed. The water level in the beck has gone down but there is plenty of evidence as to the height it must have peaked at yesterday. We had at least an inch of rain, I think.

Baby blue tits are following their parents round the canopy. They sound fine, and I think the woodpeckers have fledged (I can hear them but I have not seen them). I met a female blackcap by the steps to the stone bridge, with food for her young. She was not happy to see me.

A lone female roe deer was caught on the webcam but she was too far away to judge if she is still pregnant or not. I think she should have had her young by now but they – or it – will be well hidden.

One great tit parent is being pursued by a nearly full grown baby. The blue tits in the oak haven't fledged yet, and nor have the jackdaws. The stock doves were together on the big homemade box, but I have not noticed any sign of nesting. There are blackbirds nesting, probably a second brood, in the beech hedge.

June 8: We have had more heavy rain but the various tit families sound as if they are doing well, with lots of calling through the tree tops. The tree sparrows have hatched in the nest box, but of course we can't see how many there are. The chaffinch is singing a lot today, but I'm not sure if they have more than one brood.

The spotted flycatcher is hunting from the top of the dying greengage tree at last. I hope he will settle in the new nest box, but I must go and watch and see if he is already in there.

June 9: There was lots of noise in the southeast corner of the wood this morning. The jay family have fledged! The jackdaws have fledged as well and joined the roosting flock on the top of the hill.

The starlings have a second brood in the little owl box, which is excellent news. I haven't seen the flycatcher again today.

June 10: I went for a walk with the Geltsdale walkers in the South Tyne valley. It was rather wet to start with but improved as the day went on. Wildlife highlights included a cuckoo, a pair of curlews, oystercatchers and a lot of lapwing. There was a female merganser with three chicks swimming across rapids in the river, and we saw a dipper and grey wagtails. As we walked up through a small village we spotted a young house martin on the road, so I lifted it up onto a wall. It shook itself and took off and was instantly accompanied by the parent who escorted it to the roof. Fabulous to watch.

June 11: Cool, showery and windy today. A lot of leaf and twig debris is down from the trees but despite some strong gusts there has been no major damage.

June 12: The damp warm weather has brought out lots of flies, especially bluebottles – no doubt good nourishment for the wildlife, but rather annoying when I'm busy outside.

The tree sparrows in the box sound as if they are growing, as are the starlings in the little owl box.

June 13: There have not been many warm summer evenings for wildlife watching so I've been making the most of the sun this evening to sit (complete with blanket and jumper) in the wood to see what might be going on.

This is the time of the year I value the wisdom of my lovely Uncle Fred who advised me that no one could be a good bird watcher without learning the calls and songs. I appreciate he was right, despite my having to relearn some of the summer migrants every spring, and this will prove the point . . .

In the last five minutes I've seen a robin, great tit, jackdaw and wood pigeon. But I have heard song thrush, chiffchaff, coal tit, wren, rook, blackbird, blue tit, stock dove, greater spotted woodpecker, blackcap and possibly, a goldcrest, very faint and high in the canopy.

The half coconut filled with fat that I left on the wooden handrail of the cabin has been nibbled by something despite being upside down. I shall set a webcam to see if I can spot the culprit.

June 14: The webcam has done its job – it caught a woodpecker eating the coconut. I'm very impressed that he can get at the food when it is in that position, so I have moved it slightly and set the camera again for another night.
I saw four goldcrests flitting through the sky rocket juniper. Parents with two young, I presume. Later the pair were both hunting. I'm not sure if they are nesting yet but I would have thought so. The spotted flycatcher also returned with a bang and hit the window while chasing a fly, but it was fine.

June 15: We have a field edge upstream full of Himalayan balsam so I regularly patrol the beck and lower wood for seedlings. I found some rather tall ones today on one of the tiny islands. Fortunately they were nowhere near flowering, so I brought them up for the poultry to destroy.

A mouse was caught on the webcam last night advancing on the upturned coconut, obviously happy to share with the woodpecker.

It's hard to tell in the photos but the woodpecker may be a young one as one came twice today while I was sitting there, though it didn't land as I was too close. He flew away shouting at me.

There was no sign of its parents so it is obviously independent now.

The robin down at the cabin is extremely tame now and is actually hopping around me as I write this. I turned the coconut over and it kept coming along the handrail to tuck in. Two nuthatches came as well, not as far as the nut but happy to pick up bits the robin had dropped. A lovely half hour.

Later I saw a woodpecker feeding a young one in the apple tree, so maybe we have had two families.

June 16: The tree sparrows are now visible in the box with the webcam inside it, as they have grown enough to squash the grass lining down. We are fairly certain there are at least five young.

June 17: It's a warm, slightly humid summer day with glorious blue skies and fluffy clouds – obviously a perfect day for spiders to leave their nests. Long streamers of silk are catching the sunlight all through the wood. Stunningly beautiful.

A speckled wood butterfly has been launching himself from a fern frond in a sunny glade, but there has been no sign of a mate or rival so far.

There are some excellent photos on the wildcam of the father woodpecker feeding the young one from the fat filled coconut.

There are six young tree sparrows!

June 18: No woodland wildlife watching today. We went to Ullswater with the kayaks instead. It was very warm, but with a brisk cooling breeze, so it was a perfect day for it.

For the first time I have seen swifts drinking. Amazing creatures! On the river bank towards Patterdale there were various warblers, blackcap, willow warbler, and – a rare treat – a young kingfisher. Oh . . . and we heard one cuckoo in the distance.

June 19: A very hot day. A wonderful silence when we were eating breakfast outside. Lots of birds were singing, and the rooks and jackdaws were making their usual cacophony when, we presume, a sparrowhawk came past and it was as if the volume knob had been turned off. Absolute simultaneous silence! I have no idea how the warning spreads but it was an amazing natural event. And in the evening I heard a barking roe deer.

June 20: There were more photos on the cabin webcam of the woodpecker feeding young . . . until they knocked the coconut onto the floor. But there were no photos at all on the camera down at the bottom of the wood. I may move it over the beck because the path down the railway embankment is well trodden by something and it would be good to find out what.

I found half a dead rabbit on the path on the far bank, but it had probably just been predated by a local cat.

The dipper flew past, calling, as I reached the stone bridge. I don't think they have two broods but I will check.

The wren down there is still singing noisily, which reminds me there was a very noisy tawny owl last night. I have not heard any babies though.

[I checked later and saw that dippers do indeed have second brood, so that is good news.]

A lot of noise was coming from the laurel bush just after lunch – almost certainly a hedgehog.

June 21: It *is* a hedgehog, very probably a female with young. There is a hollow 'cave'

SPECKLED WOOD

made up among the low laurel branches at ground level and the pile of garden trimmings and slow-to-rot compost. I can't see inside but I will keep watch.

The blackbirds by the shed are feeding a third brood, and the tree sparrows are about to fledge. We are having a busy year!

June 22: All but one of the tree sparrows have gone. No parent is brooding the remaining one but it is not cold.

June 23: I've only seen four swifts at a time this year but I hope there are more around than that. There has been a big dip in the number of swallows and house martins too. It's all very sad. The second starling brood in the little owl box are growing fast though, which is excellent.

June 24: I saw a pair of curlews on the beach at Morecambe today. This is another bird that seems to have drastically dropped in numbers in recent years. We hear very few at home now.

June 25: There seem to be a huge number of jackdaws being fed by their parents. I'm not sure how many they have in a brood but there must be more families than just the residents of the two owl boxes.
The evening flight from the hilltop this evening was stunning – probably at least eighty to a hundred jackdaws and rooks – but they are harder to count than geese as they swirl and swoop above the tree tops. A very special sight.

June 26: I spent a long morning pulling up Himalayan balsam from the edge of the wood and along the beck. It can fling its seeds over fifty feet and is very invasive, especially on damp ground. It is a plant we really don't want in our wood.

June 27: We have had rain all day and it's rather chilly for June. Not a day for wildlife watching!

June 28: Another cold day for June, but I had a nice walk with Betty near Lanercost. I saw a pair of swifts – briefly – but not much else.

June 29: Rain again for most of the day. Even the roost of rooks and jackdaws have been very quiet.

June 30: The rain has stopped and it is a bit warmer but it is still very gloomy. A walk at Talkin Tarn showed that the swans have still got their seven cygnets. They have grown an amazing amount in the week.

At home some of the birds are singing again – the robin, wren and song thrush in particular. The evening flight over the wood is back up to full strength. In fact it seems noisier than ever. It's just as well we enjoy it!

JULY

July 1: We had warm sun for a short while this morning, then it was back to chilly winds and drizzle for the rest of the day. There has been no sign of froglets this year in the pond, though there were plenty of tadpoles.

The yellow flags are rather overpowering so there is less and less water space in there. There are frogs around in the garden though, and our daughter Jules found a particularly large one near the house just the other day.

All the leaf colour in the wood has melded into one dark green, the colour of high summer – in my opinion one of the least attractive times of the year, especially with no sun to cheer it up.

July 2: I went down to check the wildcams today, but one had no pictures and the other mainly had images of blackbirds and the neighbouring cats. There has been no sign of any deer for a while so I suspect we don't have young ones this year – a great pity as last year we got so much pleasure from watching the twins grow up, and then got some excellent views of all the family as the year went by

July 3: We still have two swifts, hopefully a pair, flying over the house, but since it won't be long before they migrate again I'm not confident that they have bred successfully. Last year I was lucky enough to see migrating swifts going over the wood. There were at least seventy passing over in the space of a couple of hours – a real treat.

July 4: Another extremely wet day. We went for a walk along Grange over Sands promenade and saw an egret settling into the marsh, and a heron flying low over the sea, but otherwise most wildlife was taking shelter. The lake at Sizergh Castle had a swan family with nine well grown young. It is obviously a very protected place in which to breed.

July 5: After shutting the poultry in late tonight I thought I could hear the sound of distant strumming. Then I realised it was a late flying bumble bee in the dog rose by my ear! The wild roses have been particularly good this year. Another treat!

July 6: The cygnets on Talkin Tarn are growing well; there are still seven, which is great.

I sat in the garden for an hour or so watching the skies above the house which twenty years ago would have been full of insect-eating birds. Sadly now there are only two swifts, about half a dozen house martins and swallows and a lone spotted flycatcher, although I'm still not certain that they have bred. It's a sad sign of the times.

On a brighter note the chiffchaffs are calling incessantly. I suspect they are all having second families. There are at least three or four pairs in the wood and garden.

July 7: Some sunshine at last, and a few butterflies – speckled woods in the sunny glade in front of the cabin, and red admirals and one tortoiseshell in the garden. The sunshine brought the bees back too, though sadly it didn't last all day.

July 8: A glorious proper summer day, but the highlight for wildlife was seeing a barn owl just down the road as we headed home very late in the evening. A pity it didn't find our nest box before the jackdaws did! Well, maybe next year.

July 9: At last the camera over the beck has caught a deer. There is no sign of young, and it's hard to tell from that angle whether it is the buck or the doe, but it's good to see something after such a long break.

There was a lovely specimen of a green orb-weaver spider on the side of the car today, which inspired me to start looking up other small creatures in the garden. We enjoy watching our blacktipped soldier beetles on the hogweed, but when I started to try to identify some of the hoverflies on the pink geraniums I soon gave up. I found there are about 236 species in Britain!

July 10: It looks as if a stock dove may be moving into the 'barn owl/jackdaw' box. One was sitting on its verandah for a long time today. The wood pigeon is on his third, or possibly fourth, nest in the Scots pine on the lawn. It's been a favourite place for generations of them.

July 11: A pair of bullfinches were enjoying the amelanchier berries this evening, their feather colours looking stunning in the sunlight. I know the blackbirds and thrushes love these berries, as does the wood pigeon, but it is the first time I have noticed these finches. The birds will have a more peaceful life from now on as we buried Skraedl, our fifteen year old ginger cat today, though it has been a while since he caught any!

July 12: It was a lovely day so we took the kayaks to Derwentwater. The young Canada geese are nearly grown up, but a pair of barnacle geese had one very tiny fluffy baby which they were guarding carefully. We spotted a mink on the river bank further up so they were right to be careful. Some sandmartins appear to be still nesting, though sadly a lot of the bank has collapsed recently and probably taken some nests with it. There was a lively bunch of swifts screaming between the houses at Grange, which is always a thrilling spectacle.

July 13: Baby goldcrests in the Scots pine in the wall have been calling to be fed. It's lovely to see the family has been successful. It was a fine warm day until eight o'clock when the heavens opened. Just when it was beginning to dry up a bit!

July 14: It was interesting driving south to Gloucestershire and seeing how much drier it had been down there. It still had very much the feeling of high summer there, whereas Cumbria is getting the first signs of autumn.

July 15: It was good to hear bunches of swifts swirling and calling round the roofs of Great Malvern, and more over Brean Down near Weston-super-Mare, despite the drizzle!

July 16: There were even more swifts at Nick's house near Stroud, and lots of bats around his garden in the evening. Maybe it was the first flight for the young, as he said he hadn't seen that many before.

July 17: We brought summer back with us! A glorious evening with warm sunshine and beautiful blue skies.

July 18: At last a chance to check the cameras and walk round the wood. There was a very large frog in the undergrowth over the Valentine bridge, and various photos of the roe doe on the wildcam over there. There was no sign of fawns yet, but it was good to see her. There was a busy treecreeper on the oak opposite the cabin, but on the whole the wood felt warm and sleepy.

July 19: It was cooler again today, with patchy sun, and the wind got up in the afternoon. The flycatcher is still around but there is no sign of young, or even nesting. The tree sparrows may well be having a third brood in the webcam box. It is out of focus again, presumably because they have built their domed nest of grass inside, but tonight there are some noises coming from inside it. It sounds as if the parent is possibly moving around on eggs.

July 20: It was drier than the forecast in the morning so I was able to sit out and watch the lone spotted flycatcher. Four swifts were flying around again so they have not headed south yet. Maybe the storm we had in the late afternoon will change their mind!

July 21: We headed south to Shropshire and there were many storms around us on the journey. We had heavy rain down there, but it was obvious that further south has had a much drier summer than we have.

July 22: There are many more house martins down here in Shropshire than at home, but though there are woods all around I didn't see or hear a jackdaw or rook. I quite missed them.

July 23: A glorious morning. The patch of thistles outside the Bongo was soon covered with at least six species of butterfly, and various hoverflies and beetles. A good hatching day.

July 24: Home again! It's still summer, I'm pleased to say, and the swifts are still here. Just down the road a green woodpecker flew over. I had only ever seen one once before, flying over the wood many years ago.

July 25: A lovely morning which turned gloomy and thundery. I had hoped to do a butterfly count but sadly only saw a white one in the distance. Hopefully we will get more sun later in the week.

July 26: The highlight today was a heron flying over the bridge over the Eden as we drove by. The river was very full for the time of year. I know there were some flash floods locally while we were away.

There are some faint noises coming from the webcam box but we still can't see anything, and I'm not convinced there is a third brood.

July 27: Rain, rain and more rain!

July 28: There were swifts over Brampton, so they are still around. There's no sign of them over the house though; the weather has probably been too grim for them.

July 29: I looked out of the kitchen window briefly and saw adult and young robin, two tree sparrows, two chaffinches, and a willow warbler or chiffchaff. I came through and checked the webcam and there is certainly something going on in the box.

Coming back up the M6 later from Keswick I was aware of dozens, if not scores, of swifts hunting over the motorway. Whether they were on migration or local is hard to say but it was great to see them all.

July 30: We have been down in the South Lakes today and it has been very windy but it was good to see swallows, house martins and swifts hunting between the showers, and fabulous to hear the swifts around the roof tops in Ambleside.

July 31: Very wet yet again, and rain for most of the night.

AUGUST

August 1: The robin was singing his winter song as we ate breakfast in the garden. Autumn always catches me by surprise here, and there was definitely a hint of it in the air.

A lovely day, much better than the forecast, so we went up onto Hadrian's Wall for a walk. It was good to see that a swallow had a nest on

RED KITE

a beam in the new visitor centre with at least four nearly fledged young in it.

An evening walk round the lanes at home gave us an excellent sighting of a sparrowhawk, male from the size, and we also heard a yellowhammer calling. A fine clear evening.

August 2: A trip down to Keswick where the swifts were still racing round the roofs, between the showers. This must be one of the wettest summers we have had since moving to Cumbria nearly 28 years ago; certainly the mud in the poultry run is fairly horrendous for this time of year.

August 3: Heavy rain again for most of the night and this morning. We are heading north

today so we hope for better weather for the drive. There was faint cheeping from the webcam box this morning but I still can't see what is going on in there.

August 4: We watched the gannets diving just off the shore at Stonehaven. Amazing birds! There were lots of eider duck and cormorants as well, and we also spotted oystercatchers and a turnstone.

August 6: There was a red kite flying low over the road today. They seem to be doing well in all the locations in the UK where they have been released. We had one over our house in June 2012. Whether it was a Galloway one or from the northeast it was still spectacular to see.

August 7: Home again to see that the rain has hardly let up in our absence. The poultry run is a quagmire.

August 8: There was no time to check the far camera today, but I tested the near one, replaced its batteries, and captured a photo of the neighbour's cat, which at least proves it is working.

August 9: This morning we woke up to sunshine, and it stayed fine and dry all day so we have started 'mowing' the hay meadows – which means strimming and raking the small patches on the lawn that we have left all summer.

One of the buddleia had at least two red admiral, one tortoiseshell, and some small white butterflies on it. Not many of them, but it has been a poor year. A flash of colour that may have been a comma passed by, but I'm not certain.

August 10: A group of about ten house martins have been hunting flies over the village. Hopefully they are all the local ones who may return next year and use my nesting pouches.

August 11: There were lots of birds around this morning. I was woken by a wren in full voice. The blackbirds are beginning to enjoy the rowan berries, though not in the numbers of a few years ago. I also spotted a chiffchaff/willow warbler (it was silent so I'm not sure which it was), two young robins and the first small group of autumn tits. The tawny owl said goodnight when I shut the poultry in. A good day all round.

August 12: On a walk up Gowbarrow Fell near Ullswater we saw a couple of migrating cuckoos over the plantation. There were stunningly clear views from the top thanks to the morning rain.

August 13: We took the kayaks down to Derwentwater for an evening paddle. The light was perfect and the parking was easy. We headed up the River Derwent, which we had all to ourselves, and were lucky to have four sightings of kingfishers – at least two individuals. Also a large flock of house martins was over the reed beds – so lovely to see as we have not had many at home.

August 14: The garden birds are gathering into their winter flocks and can be heard through the canopy, feeding. I suspect there will be plenty for them to eat as it has been a very wet warm summer, so good insect breeding weather. It poured again all night!

August 15: It was too damp to be outside today but while eating breakfast in the conservatory I saw young blackbirds, great, coal and blue tits, a female blackcap, the local wren and some tree sparrows. Wonderful! I don't think the nestbox has managed a third brood, but it has been a successful year for them nevertheless. The house martins are still around, but probably won't be for much longer.

August 16: I was drinking my coffee in the garden this morning and looked up to see a goshawk fly low over the wood from the north – a sighting confirmed by the cries it made to deter the rooks from mobbing it. It was the 84th species I have seen here, either in or flying over our land in the last nearly 28 years. We have had ten birds of prey including owls – a resident tawny, barn owls from time to time, an early sighting of a little owl years ago, and a shorteared owl down the lane a couple of years ago. We also have a resident sparrowhawk and buzzard, see kestrels, and have had one merlin, about 20 years ago and a lone red kite in 2012. The goshawk is a real treat though. Sadly it's unlikely to stay as our wood won't be a big enough territory for it.

Also today I followed a large hedgehog up the steps in the early evening, and watched as he vanished under the laurel bush in which I heard and saw them earlier in the year.

August 17: A glorious day after yet another wet night! The willow warbler and the chiffchaff were both singing while we ate our breakfast in the garden, their final fling before heading south. The house martins are still here, and a couple of swallows, but the swifts are long gone now.

August 18: I managed some gardening between the heavy showers but it was not a good day for watching wildlife. We went out and ordered a new pond for the moss and fern garden that is being created round the back of the house. It should all do rather well if our summers continue like this.

August 19: More rain! We're going off to Iceland and Greenland tomorrow. I may continue this there or just leave a two-week gap.

August 20: I am continuing it! Lava fields and sea cliffs in Iceland – kittiwakes, fulmars, shag, cormorant, golden plover, white wagtails and a whimbrel, and gannets and gulls and terns galore! That's a good start.

August 21: We had an amazing drive round Iceland's Golden Circle. The scenery was stunning, from lava fields through geysers, lakes and volcanoes to lush rural plains and coast.

Iceland is by its own admission short on biodiversity but we were lucky enough to see great skuas, a peregrine, baby goldeneye, fulmars, some unidentified sea diving ducks, black guillemot, oystercatchers, whimbrels calling, white wagtails, and greylag geese (which we now know were named after 'grey law', since they were discovered at the ancient and fascinating parliament at the split of the continental plates).

August 22: Wheatears, starlings, possibly flocks of redshank, more whimbrels, more ducks including one flying from the sea up river.

Another lovely drive, with a coffee stop by a fast flowing salmon river and lunch overlooking farm fields with gathering greylag, and Reykjavik in the distance over a sun-dappled bay. Beautiful!

August 23: We flew to Greenland. We saw many various gulls, a red throated diver on the reservoir behind Ilulissat, the town in which we are staying. There were flocks of snowbuntings, and possibly lapland buntings all around as we had a walk to a bench overlooking the ice fjord.

Nothing we had read had prepared us for this stunning view. It was one of the most amazing sights and sounds of my life. We were both moved to tears. After gazing for a long time we took a path round the headland, where a raven was suggesting he was rather hungry.

August 24: We went by small boat through the floes and bergs of the ice fjord to Iliminac, where we stayed in an amazing lodge overlooking the berg-filled sea.

There were many more snowbuntings, and some wheatear – one very orange, so I must check the Greenland varieties. Also more ravens, greylag geese and some pretty, soft looking, almost pink/grey gulls with pink feet, which were frequenting the cliffs, eating berries and foliage. I found out later that they were Icelandic gulls. There were five small diving ducklings on a lake. I had seen a mystery dark duck come in from the sea earlier so maybe that was the parent.

August 25: We saw a humpback whale from the shuttle boat on our return. Later we went whale watching, which was absolutely amazing. One fin whale, which was enormous, then some more humpback and two more fin.

Then innumerable humpback feeding at the head of the ice fjord inlets where the glacial river was providing endless food. Apparently a young humpback can put on 40 kilos a day. A fantastic day!

August 26: No new wildlife to report but I need to mention that we had an incredible sea kayak trip among the icebergs.

GREENLAND REDPOLL

August 27: We watched ravens on the town dump! Then saw lots of whales, humpback and fin, as we sailed south through the ice on the local ferry. There were many fulmars and arctic terns on our way. Apparently we passed near the biggest arctic tern colony in the world!

August 28: This is seriously wild Greenland, with miles between settlements. Even the second largest city in the country is very small. No more whales but plenty of sea birds, and two strings of the dark ducks passed us heading out to sea. It was dark at the ports so we saw no obvious wildlife.

August 29: Nuuk the capital of Greenland.

August 30: We saw some more humpback whales in the distance from the ship, but the highlight of the day was a good view of a baby sea eagle on a nest on a small island very near the ship. Our guide Isak, was delighted. One had flown but the other had obviously waited for us. We looked for caribou but had no luck.

August 31: Onshore the next day we saw loads of redpoll flocking like goldfinches around the wildflower seed heads. There were also wheatear, and the odd raven, of course.

SEPTEMBER

September 1: We went for a walk in Greenland's national arboretum at Narsarsuaq and saw even more redpolls, wheatears and ravens. Also a group of thrush-like birds, so far not identified, and more ravens, but fewer than in the larger settlements. We passed sheep today, in very wild country, and the odd farm.

September 2: We had a fabulous walk along the ridge above the river with views, and a picnic, in hot sun looking down on one of the huge tongues of glacier coming down from the central ice cap. More redpolls and wheatears, and a couple of ravens. There were a few sheep in the distance. It makes the terrain that Cumbrian sheep live on seem almost lush.

September 3: We're back in Iceland – to rain and wind, so there has not been much wildlife to see, though we saw a lot of seabirds, including fishing gannets, from the lighthouse at the end of the peninsula that Keflavik airport is on,.

September 4: A very wet welcome home to Cumbria. After the sparsity of what we have become used to it has been hard and somewhat overwhelming to take in all the birds in the garden.

September 5: It has poured most of the day so I will leave checking the cameras until tomorrow.

September 6: No rain this morning so it's a good chance to walk around the wood and check the cameras. The batteries in the far one have lasted the holiday. There are mainly photos of the neighbouring cats, but there is also enough to show that the roe deer has had twins again, and some badgers have been passing.

The dipper flew downstream as I came to the stone bridge, and there were various birds in the canopy. Sadly on top of the hill were the remaining prickles of a dead hedgehog. There was no way of saying how he might have died but he was out in the open. Maybe just illness. Who knows?

While logging later I realised the bird I had been listening to down by the beck was probably the dipper. I must check later. (It was – an amazing song that I had never knowingly heard before.)

September 7: After a brief dry start the rain set in for the day. Apart from the robin, who has found the first feeder of the winter that I have put out, there is nothing to report today.

September 9: There are more jackdaws than rooks in the roost at the moment, probably thanks to our owl boxes which have been providing homes for their families since we put them up earlier in the year. The great tit found the feeder today, but it is still raining a lot of the time so wildlife is taking cover.

September 10: Today I climbed Dodd with the Geltsdale fellwalkers, rather than the planned Lonscale Fell as the weather was so inclement. It was a lovely walk in the rain and mist. It's so good to be back in Cumbria!

September 11: A mainly dry day with a brisk wind, and a chance to prune the laurel and cut

ROE DEER

the grass. There are lots of different types of fungi popping up all over the place with some rather splendid ones on some of our piles of dead wood.

September 12: A dry morning and afternoon – what a bonus! I managed to get a lot done outside while listening to the robin's winter song coming from various directions, accompanied by a wren or two. We had a brilliant flying display by the jackdaws and the rooks, much higher in the sky than usual. There were a lot of red admirals around too, very pristine and lovely.

September 13: A chiffchaff was singing happily as I went out to get the poultry up for the day. I saw him later in the rowan tree outside the kitchen window. It was a lovely morning to be out in the garden, with some sunshine after an extremely wet night. The first named storm of the autumn – Aileen – has hit the country, but the winds here don't seem to be nearly as bad as they were forecast. We had more heavy showers later in the day, but the sun came out between them to cheer things up.

September 15: Camera checks showed nothing exciting. I need new batteries in the newer one, which had lots of cat photos on it! The old one seems to be working again so I have reset it in the bottom of the wood.

House martins are still flying above the house, but they may be migrants from further north. The robin has been singing beautifully on and off all day, a much more varied song than his usual winter one and very lovely to hear.

September 17: Richard and I went for a beautiful walk along the South Tyne at Lambley, then followed part of a Haltwhistle Ring walk along a ridge with fantastic views towards Cold Fell and right round to Hadrian's Wall and up towards Alston. A pair of hares in the last field completed a good day out.

September 18: The chiffchaff is still singing, but the autumn flocks of tits are building up in the wood. There were at least seven long-tailed in today's flock. They are beginning to come to the feeders now, especially the great tits.

September 19: An exquisite autumn morning, chilly but with lots of sunshine. A walk up Talkin Fell with Betty was rewarded by glorious views, with two buzzards, one being mobbed by a flock of jackdaws.

September 20: A local walk was a delight, with some lovely trees just beginning to turn into their autumn finery, the tips of the beeches looking particularly beautiful.

At home, we had the amazing sight of a mother hedgehog moving her babies from the bottom of our garden, near the lane, to a place near our shed. We saw her do three trips, but she may have done more before we spotted her.

September 22: Back to the rain again but fine enough to collect the camera from over the beck and bring it up for a good check and tidy up. There were many blank and cat shots to delete, but some fabulous deer photos, especially of this year's family. There were some reasonable badger photos too, and the odd rabbit and possible stoat as well. Pheasants, pigeons and blackbirds abound, and the odd annoying shot of the squirrel – grey of course!

September 24: Richard and I walked from Aira Force to Glenridding by Ullswater. The autumn colours are getting better by the day. We caught the steamer back and then went up to the Force. Plenty of water was coming over. From the steamer I saw a flock of about 11 merganser flying over the lake.

September 26: A very noisy grey squirrel was shouting at me by the washing line. It sounded like a cross between a red one and a duck, followed by a jay-like screech. I'm not sure I have ever really heard one before.

We had a stroll down to a local farm sale. It must feel so sad having to leave a farm like that, but the bonus for us was that there was a burger van there so we had our lunch, resisting the temptation to purchase a mini digger or some sheep hurdles while we were there!

September 27: I had coffee on the cabin verandah with a red admiral and three speckled wood butterflies enjoying the sun in the glade in front of it. There were photos of a deer and a grey squirrel on the camera over the beck, but just a blur on the old camera as it had obviously been knocked over by something. The beck was very full again after last night's rain.

September 28: A glorious autumn day. I had a fabulous walk with Betty in the fells behind Talkin. It was very soggy underfoot, but rewarded by sunshine and wonderful views. There were lots of grouse calling, and many imported red legged partridges, and an excellent view of a buzzard that took to the skies just in front of us.

The old holly tree at the bottom of the garden is now smothered with ivy and the flowers are attracting loads of insects and especially, today, dozens of red admirals in the evening sun. They were too high and too many to count properly, but a fabulous sight.

September 30: A proper autumn day, beautiful light and warm with a gentle breeze. The colours are coming on well though sadly the amalanchiers have peaked earlier than usual so the contrast against the rest of the wood and garden is lost. Many more holly trees in the wood have berries on them this year, which seems to have become an annual progression recently. I had always thought the majority in the wood were male.

OCTOBER

October 1: A drier day than forecast but the strong winds did arrive, which made it very autumnal. Most of our garden and wood is sheltered from the prevailing southwesterly wind which is nice, but lots of leaves are starting to tumble today. We hope that some will remain to provide some colour.

October 2: It's very windy today, and a large piece of the ash tree down the road broke off in a gust. The wind seemed to keep the day drier than forecast, though, giving us the chance to cut the hawthorn hedge at the end of the garden. It is a popular sparrow roost but was not occupied while we were doing it so they weren't disturbed. More red admirals have been braving the gale and enjoying the splashes of sunshine that have come through from time to time.

October 3: I had some lovely walks on the North–East coast with Jo – Alnmouth, Craster, and from Beadnell to Seahouses and back. We saw a seal in the harbour at Craster, and lots of turnstones, redshank and some curlew. Some greylag geese flew overhead. It was all very autumnal.

October 4: We had a day on Holy Island. Whooper swans were arriving from the north, and many waders and five seals were fishing along the shore. Amazingly, there were still swallows flying and feeding young on the wing near the priory – very late, I would have thought. An egret flew over as we crossed the still damp causeway. They have certainly colonised England.

October 5: The most amazing birds today were the starlings on the harbour wall in Seahouses. The light was perfect for showing off their fantastic colours, and the repertoire of the calls and songs above our head was fantastic. They were very tame and happily ate doughnut crumbs from our hands!

October 6: Another lovely day on the North-East coast, and at last we spotted some drake eider in Amble harbour, not a bird Jo would have ever seen in her home county of Cornwall.

October 7: A very interesting observation at the North Lakes Wildlife Park today. Brian the Lar Gibbon was showing off to us, Richard and I went with Will and Gem, he was swinging around and calling a lot . . . and then a rook came onto a nearby post and was obviously calling to him. It was fascinating to watch.

October 8: A lovely paddle in our kayaks on Ullswater. The colours are beginning to look perfect. Small flocks of greylag kept flying overhead.

October 9: A good gardening day, though lacking in sunshine. I did some excellent holly pruning to let in some light from the west. I'm hoping for a sunny evening to see how well it has worked.

Flocks of long-tailed tits are in the canopy but they are too high to count properly. Our morning and evening flying displays by the rooks and jackdaws are increasing. It's a wonderful sight.

There are some very late, half developed froglets in the pond with the flags, but there is not much clear water in there so I'm not sure how they will fare. I shall keep an eye on them.

October 10: A breezy day in the wood but lots of sunshine, especially after more pruning of the holly. A buzzard was enjoying the swirling wind above the tree tops, and the fungi on the woodland floor were looking especially good in the splashes of sunlight.

October 11: Torrential rain and gales all night which continued most of the day. There is lots of surface water and there have been flood alerts throughout Cumbria. Let's hope it isn't a forerunner of a bad winter.

October 12: A brighter day but still a lot of rain. I have been keeping an ear open and an eye out for winter visitors in or over the garden but it's still very quiet.

The buzzard was enjoying soaring low over the wood, and was joined from time to time by either his mate or a sibling. Wonderful to watch.

October 14: A wet and breezy walk near Orton with Richard after a lunch at Tebay motorway services. It was extremely soggy underfoot but better up on the Scar and the limestone pavement. We spotted a late wheatear which at least seemed to be flying south, and three snipe – a pair and a single.

LONG-TAILED TIT

A very kind farmer drove out from his yard on his quad bike to suggest we headed straight down his track to the road as the route he could see we were planning to take was well under water. He reckoned his farm could easily see 20 inches of rainfall in October alone!

October 15: A damp and breezy walk with the Geltsdale fellwalkers by a very full Derwentwater was rewarded by seeing a red squirrel in Lingholm woods.

October 16: An amazing spectacle this morning – a red sun and a black, then orangey yellow sky, all apparently caused by the winds of Hurricane Ophelia bringing sand from the Sahara and smoke from the forest fires in Portugal. It was all rather apocalyptic! The gale in Cumbria was not as bad as expected but Ireland suffered a lot.

October 17: A lot of small debris, dead branches, twigs and leaves have come down in the wood but there has been no obvious major damage. It helps that the wind was from the south this time, which is more sheltered for us.

October 19: A dry and bright day, with the woodpecker flying around the canopy calling a lot. A very handsome male pheasant is using the step outside our bedroom as his calling point for his territory. Fortunately he doesn't start too early in the morning!

October 20: We spotted a barn owl flying across the lane opposite our house on our way out in the car. It's good to see them around. A large high branch has torn off from an oak in the wood. Some of it has hit the ground but most is still dangling, supported by a rowan. I will look at it when the winds have died down a bit, but another gale is forecast for tomorrow.

October 21: It was not too windy in the morning so I had time to inspect the wood and start clearing leaves. The oak branch is safe for now. In the late afternoon the rain began, and the winds got up so it was time to batten down the hatches for the night.

LONG-TAILED TITS

October 22: A damp gloomy morning, but much more light has been coming into the wood because a lot of the leaves have blown down, especially from the sycamores. It turned into a

lovely evening, and there was a lot of activity in the canopy – there were certainly long-tailed tits calling, but it was still hard to do a proper count.

October 24: Another damp start to the day, but the afternoon was beautiful. I walked with Betty at Talkin Tarn. The trees were looking good with the autumn colours and there were lots of birds on the water. The swan family have raised four of their youngsters. There were many squabbling coots, and a flock of at least thirty Canada geese. Also some mallard, but nothing very unusual as far as we could see.

October 25: A lovely sunny walk with Richard by the Esk at Longtown. There was a lot of water because it had rained hard yet again the night before.

There were some small flocks of thrushes in the hawthorn hedges. Also a lot of blackbirds mainly, with a sprinkling of redwings and I think at least one fieldfare. They were all unusually quiet so it wasn't easy to tell.

October 26: I went on a fungi hunt with Val, who is a bit of an expert, round the wood but sadly a lot have gone over now. There was still a good variety, though. I need to study them more in order to name them. The dipper was singing almost constantly on the stone bridge, possibly confused by the warm sunshine coming through the trees, and there were lots of birds flitting through the canopy above our heads.

October 27: After pruning yet more holly to let some light into the wood I sat for a while on the cabin veranda. The sunshine was beautiful and the trees, especially the beech, were all looking lovely, though the leaves are falling steadily now.

The birds are beginning to come to the feeders and I saw all the tit families, plus the nuthatch, great spotted woodpecker, some chaffinches, and a pair of fighting robins . . . and a buzzard soaring overhead.

October 28: A dark and gloomy day, but with very little rain which is something to be thankful for. It got more windy as the day went on, and was dark soon after five o'clock.

October 29: A totally contrasting day. The clocks went back last night and yet the day was so bright and sunny that the evening seemed longer than last night. Richard and I went for a glorious walk along the west shore of Derwentwater.

Warm sun, beautiful colours and a blue lake – a perfect day. In the village of Grange we stood next to a sparrowhawk just over a wall, totally unfazed by us watching him. He only flew when the home owner opened the gate under where he was perching.

October 30: A day in the garden with many birds all around. Tit flocks in the canopy, woodpeckers calling, nuthatches as well, and the rooks and jackdaws circling above the wood – a proper autumn day.

October 31: A very damp miserable day, only briefly brightened by Balou, our cat, very nearly catching the grey squirrel who is getting rather bold, I will set the trap soon.

NOVEMBER

November 1: Autumn is very much here now if the feeders outside our bedroom window are anything to go by. In the space of not much more than five minutes we had great, blue and coal tits, two robins, a chaffinch, and the great spotted woodpecker. Then the grey squirrel appeared for good measure!

November 2: A stunning walk up High Pike with Betty in glorious sunshine with no wind. The views were superb in all directions, and it was good to see a lot of other people making the most of the day.

November 3: A trip to Maryport Aquarium with Judy was a successful day. The tide was in, many redshank were in the harbour, and some oystercatchers were flying overhead! The aquarium was fascinating as it is based on the creatures found in the local seas. It is amazing to think that all that goes on in the sea and estuary around Cumbria's shores! The metal shoal of herring in the entrance hall were made by Judy's blacksmith husband, John, many years ago, they are amazing.

November 4: The loop up at the RSPB reserve was a lovely place for a walk for Richard and me on a surprisingly good day. The forecast had threatened rain and we did have a stunning rainbow on our drive up there, but the rain stayed away and the sun came out. There was a large flock of about 100 fieldfare, and a birdwatcher we passed said he had seen some probably Scandinavian ring ouzel on the slopes of the fells.

November 5: Another lovely day of sunshine and no wind. I gathered lots of leaves for leaf mould, and tidied up some trees near the cabin both to improve the view and hopefully to allow space for a dangling piece of oak to swing in the next gale and come down safely.

Our mystery bird of prey flew low and fast through the wood just over the beck. It can surely only be a buzzard but it would be good to identify it for certain. A chilly end to the day. There could be a frost tonight.

November 6: A crisp morning walk all round Talkin Tarn. There were lots of Canada geese and one greylag, many coots and mallard, and just a few wigeon to brighten it up.

November 8: We had the annual trip over to Durham for the AGM of Harrison & Harrison, our family organ-building business. The colours were lovely all the way and the trees along the river by the cathedral were especially fine.

November 9: We had tree surgeons working in the wood today. Some over-extended and dead oak was cleared on the hill, and a medium sized beech was removed because it was in the wrong place. The work has made an amazing difference – there is now more light and space for some of the young rowans up there.

November 10: A sunny morning to begin gathering, sorting and splitting logs. The tree surgeons laid the brashings from the beech over the brambles at the top of the hill so they are still giving a good display of colour from the leaves and will improve the habitat as they break down.

November 11: A lovely crisp autumn day. A sunny walk round Talkin Tarn with the family, and drinks outside at the cafe while the grandchildren fed the ducks. Lovely.

November 12: Another glorious day, though it turned chilly in the afternoon. The wildlife camera over the beck had some more deer photos on it – the two young ones, and also the buck cleaning his antlers on a branch.

November 13: Dry and bright. A good day for mass leaf clearing and log splitting and stacking.

November 14: We did some more log splitting and stacking on top of the hill, making new piles to create some habitat for the next couple of years. A wren was making a noisy inspection of the beech pile almost immediately!

November 16: A wet and windy night but by nine o'clock this morning the sun was out. This was one of the loveliest days in the wood this year! There was a carpet of oak and beech leaves reflecting the ones remaining on the trees, with blue sky and bright sunshine completing the picture.

A pair of dippers were bobbing on my low brushwood dams in the beck, then they flew past me under the wooden bridge. The bottom wildlife camera had loads of deer photos, many with three in the view, and the long-tailed tits passed by in a flock of at least a dozen birds. Some more of the holly trees down by the beck have berries on for the first time. They look fantastic against the blue sky.

Richard and I spent some of the afternoon removing random trees that had grown too big on the bank by the house. At least they are big enough to log and the brashings will improve the habitat on the hill and on the bank down to the road.

WREN

November 18: A bright sunny day again so we sat down for lunch at the cabin. There was a lot going on – a flock of long-tailed tits plus blue, great and coal tits, and a tree creeper and nuthatch. A noisy wren was singing nearby and there were busy rooks and jackdaws overhead. Later I watched the grey squirrel busy in the canopy before it came down on the woodland floor. It had no idea it was being watched.

November 20: A damp morning after a very wet night, but it was brightened up by a flock of long-tailed tits coming right along the front of the house. There were at least a dozen of them but it was impossible to count them exactly.

November 21: Another horrendously wet night, so everywhere is soaking again. The beck was in full flow by the end of the afternoon, pouring over the brushwood dams and nearly flowing over the stone bridge. The forecast is for more storms tomorrow. Let us hope it has been exaggerated.

November 22: The forecast was not exaggerated. We felt rather guilty driving over Shap on the M6 and leaving Cumbria in such awful weather, with many roads being blocked in the south of the county. It was nice to see better weather south of Preston, though we know North Wales was hit badly as well.

November 23: It was mainly dry and bright in Gloucestershire, but there were cold winds from the north.

November 24: We had a glorious sunny drive north through Wales, but were greeted by an amazing hail storm on Llandudno pier. Richard braved the weather to go right round Great Ormes Head, but Liz, Chris and I just walked to the far shore and back.

November 25: There was snow overnight in Snowdonia, but then it turned into a bright and breezy day with the odd hailstorm.

November 27: Back home. A wet morning which soon brightened up into a chilly but dry day with lovely bursts of sunshine. A good day for clearing an enormous amount of leaves from ground, gutters and lower roof, much to the delight of the robin, in particular, who found lots to eat among the debris.

November 28: A bright cold and sunny day. There were more deer photos on the camera over the beck, but sadly – though rather excitingly – there were also close views of a buzzard on the woodland floor who was obviously having trouble flying. We are wondering if he is the one we have seen occasionally swooping low between the trees, and maybe he has misjudged his flight path. I will keep an eye out for him over the coming days.

November 29: There was no sign of the buzzard so hopefully he has recovered enough to fly again.

DECEMBER

December 1: My daughter Jules and I woke to a glorious morning in Grasmere, and I had a spectacular drive over Kirkstone Pass – sunshine with snow on the tops – followed by a brisk walk up Grisedale to meet her running through, in the sun, admiring icicles on the rocky spurs on the fellside. A heron was flying up the beck searching for a good place to fish.

December 2: Today was damp but rather lovely and I had a walk up High Pike with the Geltsdale fellwalkers.

December 3: Richard and I went for a glorious four mile local walk, and then did lots of logging and cleared the wood of various debris which we took to the tip. The noise of the log trolley must have inspired the dipper to sing, as he was sounding heavenly in the late afternoon.

December 4: A dry and sunny morning, perfect for admiring the tidy wood and stacking more logs. A busy day for our gardener!

December 6: Now we're in Spain! We've seen swallows, or possibly house martins, on the coast in Andulucia.

December 7: We spotted gannets off the coast at Marbella, I didn't realise they go south in the winter, and later there were bats feeding over the edge of the beach at dusk. A peregrine settled on top of one of the holiday blocks.

December 8: There were more swallows, and a blackbird singing around our apartment. There are bantams all running loose around the town near the park opposite where we are staying. One cockerel particularly enjoys crossing the fairly busy road, often on the pedestrian crossing!

December 10: An amazing overnight storm with torrential rain and strong winds.

December 11: Our rail trip up into the Spanish mountains was dramatic! The rain had washed away lots of soil and the gullies and rivers were just swirling currents of muddy water. As the sun dried up the landscape later I saw two lots of massive griffon vultures soaring overhead.

December 12: I saw a monarch butterfly in the local park – an amazing creature. It almost looked like a bat flying over.

December 13: We got back to the cold reality of Cumbria. It is warmer than it was here while we were away but there was still loads of ice in the water buckets in the hen run.

There were a lot of photos on the wildcam at the bottom – mainly deer, I think, but I must bring it up to check on a bigger screen. We had more tree felling and logging today so it will be interesting to see if it has disturbed the deer at all. It doesn't seem to have done so in the past.

December 14: There was cold heavy rain nearly all day. The evening dried out but then there was a hard frost on everything. A pair of tawny owls were calling to each other in the trees over the hen run.

December 15: Warnings on the radio when we woke of sheet ice all over Cumbria, causing many minor accidents on the roads. Also a report of snow on the hills.

December 17: Richard and I drove down to Keswick, where it was a bit warmer – though damp, misty and windy down by Derwentwater. The clouds lifted a bit so we could see the snow on the fells.

December 19: Rachel Gibson mentioned yesterday that she may have had a female merlin drinking from her pond, and when Richard was walking down the lane opposite, he was following a bird of prey flying along the hedgerow – not a sparrowhawk, which he would recognise, he said, but more like a kestrel, though it was not flying like one. So maybe it was the merlin again?

December 20: We were up on Hadrian's Wall today. There was a lot of low cloud, so visibility was poor, but I did hear fieldfares. Earlier, in the morning, a very fast bird of prey flew round the end of the house and up the bank. I strongly suspect it was the merlin.

December 22: At least ten long-tailed tits were on the feeders, so busy it was hard to count them. There was a nuthatch and great spotted woodpecker as well, and the grey squirrel, sadly.

December 24: A bright windy morning, fairly mild for the time of year, and it seems to be getting lighter already. The old rotten alder has finally come up by the roots down by the stone bridge. It makes a lovely feature along the far bank.

December 26: It's drier, and much brighter today. Our beck had flooded yesterday, and the stone bridge and the dams had gathered a lot of fresh debris. There were a lot more deer photos! A walk by the Solway marshes was beautiful in the afternoon light, with flocks of curlews and calling redshank around us. There was even some warm sun – a faint hint of spring!

December 27: A glorious crisp day, with turkey sandwiches in the sunshine on the cabin verandah. There was possibly a male merlin flying below us, so fast that it was very hard to judge its size. But it had a very blue back, and seemed too small for a sparrowhawk.

December 28: A beautiful day for a drive into the Lake District, with sunshine and snow on the tops. Some mergansers were fishing on Rydal Water, and buzzards and fieldfares were flying overhead. One wren was singing valiantly in a warm patch of bracken, and a robin was singing in Dora's field in Rydal village.

December 29 - January 1: We were up in Deeside where it was very icy though there was not much snow..

JANUARY 2018

January 2: Some amazing work has been done by our tree surgeon while we have been away. He has cleared holly in all the right places, and it is going to be a great improvement.

There were seven tree sparrows on the fat feeder this morning. They are doing rather well.

January 3: A named storm, Eleanor, hit the county last night, with 100 mph gusts on top of the Pennines. There was no major damage in the wood, just a lot of small debris brought down, and hopefully the last of the leaves. A reasonable day until late afternoon when the rain returned.

January 5: A bright day. A large flock of long-tailed tits appeared on the feeders twice today. Lots of logs have been split, mainly from the dead greengage tree.

January 6: A lovely walk with Richard, Betty, Dick and Val on Hadrian's Wall at Thirwall, with sunshine and snow showers. We came home to find our 16-year-old cat, Balou, had died suddenly, but peacefully, near his hunting ground, possibly while trying to catch a mole. I suspect there will be many more rabbits around this spring, because he was a great hunter and was still catching mice in his last days.

January 7: A walk in Borrowdale with the Geltsdale fellwalkers in glorious sunshine. It was icy underfoot, but crisp and beautiful. We had the bonus of seeing a stoat in his full winter ermine, hunting in moss covered boulders in the woods above Rosthwaite – a rare sight in England.

January 8: Another very cold but sunny day, good for clearing and burning some of the brashings from the tree surgeons' work, although we plan to leave a lot of it for wildlife habitat. We watched a large number of tree sparrows again on the feeder.

ROBIN

January 9: There were plenty photos of the roe deer on the wildcam, so obviously we haven't put them off with the work we have been doing in the wood.

We mended some of the fallen and damaged nest boxes today. One – hanging precariously from one corner – was brought as hand luggage by a student from New York State who came to stay with us on a school exchange about twenty years ago. It has been stuffed full of grass over the years, and has certainly been a major factor in the rise of the tree sparrow population in the garden. They use it at least twice a year.

I looked out of the front window at dusk and spotted that the wrens are using it as a winter roost, so they are obviously happy with the fact it is now hanging correctly rather than at the jaunty angle it was before.

There were at least six in there, but it was hard to count as they kept popping in and out. I will try to check it properly tomorrow evening.

January 11: A pair of house sparrows have been looking at the sparrow terrace nest box on the front wall of the house. They often nest in the ivy of a nearby tree but it would be good to see the box being used by them.

A pair of great tits have used one end of it in previous years. The woodpecker has been drumming a lot today.

We have converted one of our larger boxes into apossible site to tempt him, but he will probablyuse one of our old birch or pine trees to nest in as usual.

January 13: At least ten blackbirds have been on the feeders – a good mix of male and female with, I suspect, some migrants from the north. The woodpeckers are drumming all over the wood, and it sounds as if there is a new drumming spot in the northwest corner.

GOLDFINCHES
and
SISKIN

January 15: Gem found a hibernating hedgehog on the bank, not very well buried but fast asleep. It didn't wake even though it rolled down the hill a bit, so she put it back and covered it more thoroughly. I will keep an eye on it but think it will be all right.

January 16: A night of heavy snow further north just over the border has blocked the M74, which is unusual. We had some snow here but not much.

January 17: Gales have been building up today. The overnight forecast is not good.

January 18: There has been no damage from the wind, but I think it was nowhere near as bad as had been forecast. There was a lot of rain in the early hours, but it soon turned to snow – very wet snow. A sunny morning.

We might have two singing dippers on the beck, but I'm not certain. There was one singing downstream from the high bridge, and possibly another in the usual place by the stone bridge, which was rather exciting.

January 20: Nothing new on the cameras but a lovely sunny, though chilly day. The snowdrops are showing on the far side of the beck. I only planted them a few years ago but they are spreading well.

The rook and jackdaw roost was busy in the late afternoon, and I am still watching to see any first signs of nest building. I don't think it will be very long now. The robin is singing more – maybe his spring, rather than his winter, song. I stacked a lot more logs.

January 21: A lot of wet snow fell again today. The long-tailed tits are really appreciating the fat feeders. It is still impossible to count them all, but there are at least ten.

January 22: Our pair of buzzards have been performing dramatic flights over the canopy ofthe wood today, possibly courtship flights. I need to read up on such events.

January 23: I just mentioned to Richard yesterday that we hardly ever get goldfinches here, but was rewarded today by a large flock, possibly at least ten, of them chattering in the trees down the garden. One paused long enough In the sunshine on the very vertical silver birch to be positively identified. Earlier in the day one of the grey squirrels was trying to get the cock pheasant to play with him. Very bizarre, but very funny.

January 25: A pleasant day, with lots of bright sunshine, and our wonderful dipper singing loudly down on a branch in the beck. Lots of woodpecker drumming as well, and catkins forming on the hazels. Early signs of spring!

January 26: Another nice day, I had a short walk over in Northumberland to a waterfall with Val, working out how to do a day's walk up the River Irthing to it sometime.

January 27: I was woken by the singing of the song thrush, with backing percussion from the woodpecker. Wonderful, a real sign of spring. Lots of birds – including tree sparrows and long-tailed tits – have been on the feeders so it made a good count for the RSPB garden bird watch. A greedy grey squirrel came and ate a lot of the food but I'm pleased to say we successfully trapped it later – the first of the year.

January 28: The catkins on the hazels are fantastic this year. Many of our trees were planted by the red squirrels in earlier times. It would be lovely to get them back again.

January 30: Rather mild today, so I am hoping it is not warm enough to wake the hedgehog!

January 31: Torrential rain in the night, rather than the snow that was forecast, but the morning brought a bitter northerly wind. I suspect the hedgehog will be sleeping well after all.

FEBRUARY

February 2: A glorious day with hints of spring. No cold wind and lots of sunshine. The only creature caught on camera was a large black collie. I didn't recognise it. The wigeon on Talkin Tarn were mobbing the coots whenever they came up with weeds. I had not seen that before.

February 3: We had a wonderful walk with the Geltsdale fellwalkers up to Crammel Lin

waterfall on the River Irthing just over the border into Northumberland. Some light snow but otherwise a reasonable day. It was muddy in places but so worth it. The previous night's rain had filled the river so it looked especially spectacular.

February 4: A beautiful day. Perfect weather for building a new hide down near the beck. I'm sure the woodpecker was drumming in reply to the sound of the drill!

February 5: Some more hide building, and log throwing up the hill from the beck. We need to get as much done as possible before the breeding season starts in earnest in the wood. There are lots of birds calling and beginning to sing already.

February 6: We found at least two inches of snow when we woke up, but it soon stopped and melted a bit. I followed grey squirrel footprints for a long way round the wood. It had stayed on the path all the way down to the beck, then avoided the bridge to cross, but then continued to the old fallen tree before heading up into the canopy.

February 8: The blackbird has just started to sing near the house, so we have decided to postpone any more work on the holly in the wood until the autumn.

February 9: I'm so sad to say there is a dead roe deer on the bank on the opposite side of the beck. It can only have died in the past few days but a lot of it has been eaten, and pulled around by scavengers. I have set a camera nearby to see if we can capture any activity. It is hard to tell how it died but it might have been hit by a train.

February 10: I was delighted to see the dipper, actually surfing down the stream from one perch to another, then singing. Also our pair of mallard have returned today, though they flew away when they saw me. We have set the wildcam to watch the deer carcass.

February 11: The carcass has been dragged further down towards the beck but for some reason nothing was captured on the camera. I have reset it and got the other one working – video and audio too – so may be more successful next time. There was a lot of water in the beck again, and a little fresh snow in the wood that soon melted. A large flock of sparrows or goldfinches was high in the canopy. They were very noisy but hard to spot in the bright sunshine.

February 13: There have been no obvious signs of life round the deer carcass, and nothing on the cameras. It was hard to look for footprints as there was a fresh fall of snow which melted quickly just as I got to the site.

February 14: There was another sprinkling of snow overnight, but it was a lovely bright morning. There was no sign of activity on the carcass last night, but plenty of action on the birdfeeders, with at least ten long-tailed tits, a similar number of tree sparrows, the woodpecker pair, and the usual selection of blackbirds, robins, dunnock and the cock pheasant. Also a male bullfinch and a couple of chaffinches.

February 15: A cold bright day with a brisk wind from the northeast. The first daffodil is out down the road, on a sunny southwest facing bank, and the crocuses on the front lawn have spread even more from the few I put in nearly thirty yearsago. We just need more morning sunshine to make the flowers open out!

February 16: Yesterday's request for sunshine was answered! The crocuses look amazing, although they are not all out yet. I did two laps of Talkin Tarn one with Betty and the other with Val. The morning one was bright and we enjoyed watching the wigeon bullying the coots for the weed they bring up.

Later it was warm enough to have lunch out on the café balcony, watching the adult swans trying to drive their family away ready to start again this year. I was obviously mistaken earlier in the year when I thought they only had four of the seven cygnets remaining as they still seem to have all seven. Excellent parenting.

February 17: Another bright sunny day with the odd shower. The birds are beginning to sing sporadically. The grey squirrel was busy with sticks up at the barn owl nest box. I wonder what the jackdaws will think if he takes up residence.

February 18: I'm not sure why I'm failing to get the wildlife camera to work. There is evidence of more activity on the deer carcass but there are no photos to show what is happening. It has been a mainly dry day, with more birds beginning to sing. The song thrush and two of the blackbirds are really getting underway.

February 19: Betty and I had a muddy walk round Hayton woods but were pleased to hear that the birds are beginning to sing there as well. We came home to find our mistle thrush

GREAT TIT

starting his spring campaign down in the wood. A pair of goldcrests were on the rowan outside the kitchen window, and it was good to see them – and hear them, as hearing them makes it easier to imprint their calls into my head.

February 20: A glorious warm sunny morning. I saw the dipper surfing on thebeck and at least three goldcrest squabbling near the cabin, and heard the woodpeckers calling and drumming all over the wood.

February 21: Some pictures on the wildcam show crows on the deer carcass, and also a deer coming to look at it. Curiosity or mourning? Who knows?

The grey squirrel is busy in the canopy, and the blue tits are investigating the big nest box on the oak tree. A song thrush is singing in the southwest corner of the wood, and there is a lot of woodpecker and nuthatch activity. Another lovely dry sunny day.

February 23: A large black and white dog wearing a muzzle has been filmed on the carcass, along with a busy crow, and some tiny night creature. A deer filmed two days ago is a male. It looks like a young one but I can't be certain.

February 24: A fox has been caught on the camera – the first we have seen here for a very long time. Another cold dry day, with winds from Siberia in the forecast.

February 26: The days are getting noticeably longer but also noticeably colder at the moment.

We had numerous snow flurries this morning, and the east wind is getting up.

The chaffinches have started to sing. There are at least two males, one near the house and one near the cabin.

Six female pheasants came down the bank by the house this morning, but there was no sign of our male, who we call Balthazar, with them. He turned up later, though, fighting his reflection in the window.

February 27: We have had snow overnight, but not as much as we expected. There is a bitterly cold wind from the east but at least the sun shines between snow showers so it all looks very lovely.

February 28: There was at least four of inches of snow this morning and the showers are still hurrying in on the bitterly cold east wind. It's no good for looking for animal tracks in the wood because the snow is too deep, and fresh snow soon covers them again.

Balthazar has been snuggled up to the window, too cold even to peck at his reflection. We had two more inches of snow by lunchtime.

It is so peaceful, with no traffic, and the birds are saving their energy as much as possible. A neighbour's dog was caught on the wildcam – as was the neighbour and his small son!

MARCH

March 1: There's nearly a foot of snow now, so there are lots of birds at the various feeders, and the poultry spent last night all snuggled up in the hen house for warmth, the ducks having gone in through the pophole to join the chickens.

It is very quiet because there is hardly any traffic as the roads are virtually impassable. The locals agree this is the longest, deepest fall of snow for many years.

March 2: Strong winds last night scattered tree debris all over the snow, even filling old footprints with leaves. It all looks rather beautiful.

A juniper fell victim to a combination of snow and wind, which is rather sad as it was a popular nesting site for one of our blackbirds, and sometimes the long-tailed tits. There has been no more snow today but the wind got up again in the evening.

March 3: There was nothing on the wildcam but I suspect that's because it was too cold for it to work. The lady pheasants came again – just three today but a lovely variety of shades of brown.

We saw a fantastic buzzard a couple of days ago, a stranger round here, with a lot of white on his underwings. The rooks were not impressed and soon saw him off.

We transformed our drive into a mini Cresta run for sledging today,. It went all the way down our drive and round the corner to the bottom of our neighbours' drive as well. Great fun.

March 4: We had more exciting sledging, but on the wildlife front the most interesting thing, unfortunately, was watching a grey squirrel lining her drey with stuffing from an abandoned teddy in the wood. She was busy all day. Not good news really.

March 5: We woke to find deer footprints all over the top of the drive, I followed them over the hill and all round the wood. They had obviously had a busy night. Deer jump the beck, but pheasants, cats and either a dog or a fox are happy to use the high bridge. The snow is still melting but lots is still lying. A lovely morning with a hint of spring.

March 6: There was an amazing video and photos on the webcam today, of the grey squirrel taking the kapok stuffing out of the old teddy for its drey. It's not often I laugh out loud in front of the computer when I'm on my own in the office, but I did watching that!

March 7: The hide is coming on well down by the beck. I have started to plant snowdrops on the bottom steep bank where the holly has been cleared. It it will be a long job, but worth it.

March 9: Yesterday and today have again been sunny and quite springlike, and the hide Richard has built down by the beck is finished. It will be amazing fun. I spent a long time on the cabin veranda watching and listening to various species of birds. It looks as if the long-tailed tits have mostly survived the cold spell. The grey squirrel came onto the roof and to the coconut feeder. I gave it rather a shock when it made eye contact with me.

March 10: A damp and gloomy day, feeling much colder than it really is. I sat in the hide for a bit but it was too chilly to linger. The rooks are building new nests as well as repairing and redesigning old ones. I will try to count them in a week or two.

March 11: A sunny bright day, positively warm in the sunshine for a short walk with Richard by Derwentwater.

Here, the wren likes the rough dams in the beck. There seems to be plenty to eat on them, and they are possibly warmer than the surrounding woodland. I watched for a while from the hide, and also saw a goldcrest busy in the holly that overhangs the beck down there. I think we have at least two pairs.

A female grey squirrel was successfully trapped today, probably the one that has been making the cosy drey near the house.

We sat in the hide for about an hour from 5.30pm and were rewarded by four female pheasants, in various colours, crossing the Valentine bridge and wandering along the far side of the beck. A song thrush and a wren saluted the dusk with some lovely singing.

March 12: There were at least two chaffinches singing in the garden, and another one down near the beck. Gem and I planted loads more snowdrops on the steep bank, and moved about six small self–seeded oak trees from the garden to the wood, on the bank and the lower level. It will give them a sporting chance.

March 13: We trapped a male grey squirrel today, so a couple more traps have been set near the boundary with the neighbouring wood.

There is no sign of the dippers on the beck again. I have not seen them since the snow so I hope they are all right.

March 14: A day out at Silloth with Judy and Richard. There were large flocks of geese on the Skinburness marshes, and oystercatchers and curlews along the coast. Also the usual turnstones along the sea wall, busy feeding.

March 15: There were more strong winds overnight. The ground and pond are full of leaves again despite being cleared up on Monday. Sturdy crocuses of all colours are braving the weather and popping up all over the place, some very obviously self seeded.

March 16: The wind is even stronger today, and I have had to rescue stuff blown all over the garden, and fish even more leaves out of the new pond. It's too dangerous to go round the wood today, with so much large debris coming down. I think the chiffchaff needs to stay in the south for a while yet.

March 17: A strong wind again today, probably another Helm wind, accompanied by hail and snow showers. It didn't get above freezing all day even though there were frequent glimpses of the sun.

March 18: More snow, and a strong Helm wind, made it very cold indeed, but it didn't stop the rooks getting on with their nest building, and squabbling over the best sticks!

March 19: A lovely day. The wind has subsided quite a lot so it's safe to be out in the garden.

March 20: We had a lovely drive through the Borders, ending up on Holy Island. A glorious springlike day, with warm sun and a light breeze, and the sea was looking lovely. There were many waders on the shore, a couple of curlews, and bartailed godwits and redshank in greater numbers. Eider duck were on the sea, and then turnstones on the beach on the coastal side of the island. We also saw two barn owls flying over the rough grass on an inland wetland, and a group of grazing roe deer near the dunes.

March 21: We woke on Holy Island to a dry morning, but it's cloudy and windy again. We had a lovely long walk through farmland and dunes, then back along the coast. We saw roe deer, and lots of birds including teal, a female golden eye, pairs of shelduck and shoveler and numerous waders, bar tailed godwit, sanderling, and grey plover. It turned wet and windy in the afternoon.

March 22: A glorious sunny, fairly calm morning, really pleasantly springlike in the sunshine. We had another lovely walk along some more of the coast. We spotted no new birds though, but I did have a splendid view of a peregrine falcon over the car on our drive home.

March 24: The dippers are still here. I got wonderful sightings of them from the new hide. There are three, almost certainly one female as

DIPPER

th e other two keep singing and displaying on the stone bridge and the little dams. They all do a lot of flying up and down, calling as well, and we had close views of them surfing, feeding, and swimming under the water. An amazing morning.

March 25: A cooler day but still plenty of sunshine. The song thrush and the blackbird are now competing loudly with each other as to which can sing the loudest. Richard and I had a lovely walk on the edge of the Pennines on a bird reserve, where lapwings and curlews were displaying loudly.

March 26: A couple of days ago I cleared some of the irises that have virtually filled our small wildlife pond. This morning, amazingly, there was already some frogspawn in it despite a lightfrost last night. More appeared later in the day. Very surprising.

Also today I heard the first chiffchaff at last. I hope the snow forecast for the weekend doesn't send him south again.

 I had delightful views of the dipper again from the hide. I was down there early today, and also saw a grey wagtail. I have seen one before in the garden or wood, but they are uncommon, and I was able to watch it for quite a while as it worked its way upstream.

As the sun shone warmly on the crocuses in the afternoon I noticed they were being visited by the first honey bee of the year. The female blackbird has been taking the soggy leaves from the pond to line her nest in the shrubs on the bank. I will never fail to be amazed how some birds can build such wonderful intricate structures with their beaks.

March 27: The chiffchaff is singing well now, as are the chaffinches. A lovely sunny day, but with the occasional cold shower.

March 29: I spoke with Rachel Gibson from the far end of the village today who had pictures on her phone of a hawfinch that they saw earlier in the year. A pity it didn't come down here!

March 30: While we were visiting Judy in hospital I spotted a male blackbird feeding a large healthy fledged youngster. Considering the weather we have had this spring it is amazing to see it has survived. There must be somewhere sheltered near the hospital.

March 31: Balthazar, our resident pheasant, has started to charge our bedroom window by running at it down the hill. I'm hoping he won't concuss himself.

There was another large and handsome cock pheasant around yesterday. He had no white collar so it was easy to tell them apart. Maybe the competition has made Balthazar more aggressive.

Two red legged partridges walked down our front steps while I was standing by the window. I know they are reared locally for shooting but hopefully these will settle in our wildlife home and raise a family. The jackdaws are making a lot of knocking noises in the barn owl box. Thereare obviously not going to be owls in there this year.

APRIL

April 1: We had snow as promised but it didn't settle in the garden, just up on the hills. The pair of bullfinches have been around a lot so I hope they nest. At least two chiffchaffs are now singing, and there are goldcrests near both the house and the cabin so hopefully we have at least two pairs of them.

April 2: Cold and wet, with a strong wind blowing most of the day. Not a day to watch wildlife except through the window.

April 3: A chilly morning with some sleet but in the afternoon the sun came out and it almost felt like spring. Another grey squirrel has been caught in our wood today, and even better news, a red one has possibly been spotted at the other end of the village.

April 4: Cold, with persistent rain, creating mud everywhere again just as we thought it was drying up.

April 6: A lovely spring day with some warmth in the sun at last. We headed down to Borrowdale for a couple of nights. There were lots of geese on the Derwent – greylag, canada and barnacle.

We looked for the kingfisher on a walk along the bank but there was no sign. There was a green woodpecker calling loudly up the valley though.

April 7: A dry morning but rain was in the forecast so we set off for a walk from our hotel in good time. The green woodpecker was still calling, and we heard drumming from a great spotted woodpecker in the distance. The rain arrived but it was not as heavy as forecast so our walk was still rather lovely. We caught the bus over Honister pass and back by Whinlatter – all very atmospheric with the clouds low over the mountains.

April 8: A beautiful morning with mist low over Derwentwater, some snow still lingering on Skiddaw and a wonderful blue sky. We paddled the kayaks from Kettlewell Bay up the river.

There were still no kingfishers, but we saw various ducks and geese and a pair of piedwagtails. The river bed had changed again in the winter storms so it was interesting to navigate.

We got home to find many more plants flowering, including the forsythia which was hardly out when we left. It shows how much the weather is warming up at last.

We think we have spotted where the buzzard is nesting in the wood. There was a lot of wing flapping in the tree tops.

April 9: We sat on the cabin veranda to watch for the buzzard but saw no sign. There was a great deal of other bird activity – chiffchaff, great and blue tits, dunnock, robin and stock dove to name a few – but most exciting was a mistle thrush nest at virtually eye level in a fork of an ivy clad sycamore growing up from the next level down.

April 10: What a contrast to yesterday! Cold wind and rain, and very gloomy, but a fantastic dawn chorus, despite the fact that most of the summer migrants are not here yet.

I heard lots of blackbirds, and the song thrush was loud and clear which was a relief as I had not heard him for a while. Hopefully he is raising a family. The dipper flew upstream when I checked the cameras, but there was no sign of any deer.

April 11: Another cool windy day, but dry. I found the first fly of the summer in the conservatory, so it must be warming up, although it doesn't feel like it. The nuthatch is calling a lot now, as are the tree creepers. I'm just waiting now for some more summer migrants. I found a dark green spotted egg shell under the main rook nests, so maybe the young are hatching. We shall see!

THE END

WOODY GLEN